Original title:
Paths through Pine Needles

Copyright © 2025 Creative Arts Management OÜ
All rights reserved.

Author: Elias Marchant
ISBN HARDBACK: 978-1-80567-304-0
ISBN PAPERBACK: 978-1-80567-603-4

## The Call of the Forest's Heart


The trees talk gossip, oh so loud,
Squirrels in shades, they gather a crowd.
In search of acorns, they leap and bound,
While I just trip on roots underground.

The fungi dance in polka dots,
Sending my shoes to untold spots.
Nature's comedy is on display,
As I try to follow, I sway away.

## Tresses of Twilight Underfoot

Twilight curls like a mischievous cat,
I step on a branch, imagine that!
The ground is a carpet of needles and cheer,
My foot does a tango with a bushy fern near.

Owls hoot laughter from branches high,
While I dance awkwardly and sigh.
The forest floor giggles as I make my way,
On this wild adventure, I feel like a play.

## A Dance with the Whispering Pines

The pines are whispering secrets, oh dear,
As I try to listen, they nudge me near.
A misstep here, a slip there,
It's a clumsy waltz, but who would care?

A chipmunk chuckles, a branch gives a creak,
As I spin like a whirlwind, feeling so meek.
Nature's ballroom full of quirky thrills,
With every misstep, the laughter spills.

## Embraced by the Pine's Green Veil

In a veil of green, I trip and twirl,
A leaf in my hair adds to the whirl.
The breeze teases gently, what a fun game,
With each little tumble, I shout out its name.

The forest is a stage, and I'm its clown,
Every branch whispers, 'You'll never drown.'
So I leap and I giggle, bark flying all around,
In this woodland circus, joy is always found.

## The Cradle of Shoots and Shadows

Tiny sprigs poke through ground,
Whispering secrets, not a sound.
Beneath the trees, squirrels debate,
Who gets the best acorn plate.

Lively ants march in a line,
Forming conga, oh so fine.
Pine needles rustle with a grin,
Nature's laughs, a cheeky win.

## Where the Pine Cones Await

Pine cones gather in a heap,
They're plotting while we're asleep.
With a wink, they start to roll,
Dancing jigs, they reach their goal.

A pine cone crowned sits up tall,
Proclaiming joy, he loves the ball.
The others chuckle, shake their bristles,
Making jokes about a nest full of thistles.

## Among the Tall Sentinels

Giant pines stand straight and proud,
Chatting softly, drawing a crowd.
With branches waving like a hand,
They tease the travelers on their land.

Beneath their shade, a rabbit hops,
Sneaks a peek, then playful stops.
Who knew that beneath such might,
Woodland jokes take joyful flight?

## The Hushed Murmur of Nature

A breeze whispers through the trees,
Gathering giggles with such ease.
The grass tickles as you walk,
As daisies join in silent talk.

A woodpecker joins the fun,
Tapping rhythms, beats run.
In the hush, life laughs anew,
Winking at me and you too.

## The Lure of the Woodland Mist

A squirrel wore a tiny hat,
He danced around, and oh, how fat!
With acorn snacks, his grand buffet,
He twirled beneath the light of day.

The trees all whispered, rustling leaves,
Confiding secrets, sharing thieves.
A rabbit laughed, with bouncing hop,
As branches tickled, never stop.

The fog rolled in, a sneaky guest,
It made us all a little stressed.
A deer came tiptoeing, quite absurd,
Rigged up in vinyl, how he blurred!

So if you wander down this lane,
And hear a giggle or a strain,
Just know that many a forest gnome,
Calls this wild place their second home.

## In the Bosom of the Evergreens


The pines were up to silly tricks,
With branches swaying, doing flips.
A pine cone fell — oh what a sight!
It landed on a bird mid-flight.

The owls were hooting their own tune,
While raccoons staged a goofy croon.
A hedgehog donned a funky tie,
And raised a glass to acorn pie.

The shadows played a game of tag,
While mushrooms danced, a real brag.
The mosses giggled soft and sweet,
As critters played their own round of fleet.

So if you hear the crackling fun,
In needles soft where critters run,
Join the party, don't be shy,
In evergreen groves, the laughs fly high!

## Secrets Beneath the Canopy

In a land where squirrels plot,
And raccoons steal a lot,
I found a treasure chest,
Full of nuts, oh what a jest!

The owls laugh with glee,
While the mice sip their tea,
Whispers of mischief loom,
Underneath the leafy room.

A fox shows off his tricks,
While the rabbits throw some kicks,
With acorns flying high,
As everyone passes by.

Secrets swirl like dandelion fluff,
With every chase, it's never enough,
Under the towering trees,
Life's a rollicking breeze!

## Footsteps Lost in the Forest

I wandered with my hiking boots,
But tripped on roots, oh what hoots!
The trees chuckled in delight,
As my journey took a flight.

A deer peeked through the greens,
Holding an air of regal teens,
While birds critiqued my stride,
All I could do was bide.

With every twist and turn I take,
I bump into a sleepy snake,
Who snaps awake in a fright,
Wishing for some peace tonight.

Yet in this tangled maze I roam,
These woods have truly become home,
With laughter echoing wide,
In this forest, my pride!

## Echoes of the Silent Wood

In the hush of leaves that sway,
A giggling frog leaps into play,
While crickets compose their song,
I join in, where I belong.

Beneath the trees so tall and grand,
A turtle gives a wave, oh so planned,
With whispers filling the air,
Nature's joke—do you dare?

Every shadow holds a grin,
As chipmunks plot to spin and win,
In this arena dark and lush,
Where even the quiet has a rush.

Echoes bounce from trunk to trunk,
Life's funny, just ask a skunk,
With laughter, we all should be,
In this wood of jubilee!

## Beneath the Needle-Laden Sky

Underneath the spiky green,
Where pinecones fall like they're mean,
I play hide and seek with fate,
Not knowing it's getting late!

A squirrel waves a cheeky paw,
Staring at me in awe,
While bees zoom past in strings,
Chasing laughter that joy brings.

With every step, I hear a crack,
A rabbit in a hasty track,
Who snickers as it bounds away,
While I tumble in the fray.

Beneath this distant, comfy dome,
I've found a new kind of home,
Each twig, each laugh, each sigh,
Turned this forest work to play!

## The Breath of the Woodland

In the woods where squirrels play,
Trees whisper jokes through the day.
A bear in a hat, oh what a sight,
Trying to dance, what a silly fright.

Rabbits giggle in a row,
Stepping lightly, moving slow.
With every hop, a chuckle flows,
Finding acorns hidden below.

Frogs croak tunes, a band on the rise,
To the rhythm of buzzing firefly tries.
They sing about a tree's shave,
And how it missees a leafy wave.

When rain tickles soft like a tease,
A wet dog spins with utmost ease.
Roots shuffle, trying to keep dry,
Only to trip when they say goodbye.

## Murmurs in the Thicket

Mice tell tales of cheese so grand,
While hedgehogs form a rock band.
Each note a squeak, each beat a thump,
A concert held right near the stump.

Pine cones tumble, rolling away,
Woodpeckers laughing, come what may.
A dance-off starts with just one toe,
Who knew that trees could steal the show?

At twilight hour, the crickets join,
Ticking away, they won't disappoint.
Chirpy jokes and jigs abound,
While leaves swirl and twirl around.

Fireflies flash in a wink, they tease,
Swirling through shadows with utmost ease.
"Catch me if you can!" they gleefully shout,
As the woodland giggles, without a doubt.

## Veins of Green in the Stillness

Beneath tall trees, the ferns do sway,
A caterpillar leads the ballet.
With a flip and a flop, oh what a twist,
Joining in cheer, the mushrooms insist.

The sun tickles leaves with a bright grin,
As a turtle, slow, tries to spin.
He trips on a root, oh what a case,
Looking quite silly in his slow-paced race.

Snakes in shades of green do slink,
Making patterns as they slink and blink.
"Where to next?" they chime with glee,
Planning adventures, just wait and see!

In the hush, a giggle starts to grow,
As ants parade in a tiny row.
"Did you hear the one about the bee?"
Buzzing and laughing, they just can't flee.

## Starlit Glimmers on Moss

Where moonlight paints with a silver brush,
A raccoon stumbles, causing a rush.
Trips on a stone, falls in a pile,
Emerging with moss, oh what a style!

The night is bright, with shadows that dance,
Fireflies flicker, giving a chance.
To catch a glimpse of wonders anew,
As owls glance down, feeling the queue.

Silly shadows twirl on the ground,
As the night creatures gather 'round.
What a sight, this woodland plight,
Singing with laughter till first light.

Moss cushions the whims of the night,
Every critter joins in with delight.
"Hey, were you dancing?" a fox inquires,
"Just moving with flair, fueled by our cheers!"

## Symphony of the Subtle Fronds

A squirrel dropped his nut, oh dear,
A meltdown caused a ruckus here.
The birds chirp out a lively tune,
While ants march like a tiny platoon.

The breezes dance like they're all in sync,
As pinecones fall, we all must think.
With each soft crunch, the forest giggles,
Nature's punchline, it just wiggles!

## Secrets Within the Sylvan Silence

Why did the tree blush? Who knows,
When the woodpecker started a show,
Frogs croaked jokes, they thought were grand,
While turtles laughed, so slow and planned.

A raccoon in shades pranced with flair,
Spinning round like a mini bear.
Deer played poker, the stakes were high,
Until one tripped, oh how they did cry!

## Treads of the Timeless Forest

Beneath the snow, a cat did freeze,
His fluffy paws couldn't take the tease.
A fox said, 'Don't worry, it's just a game,'
As snowflakes fell, they looked the same.

The rabbits raced, a thumping affair,
But tripped on branches that lingered there.
With laughter echoing through the glade,
Nature's jesters, they never fade!

## Hushed Conversations of the Pines

The owls whisper secrets—who knew?
While pine needles wink, 'How do you do?'
A chipmunk scurries, collecting a stash,
Riddles him round, going quite fast.

The pines exchange stories, oh what a mess,
'That squirrel, I swear, it's anyone's guess!'
Like gossipy friends in a café chat,
Even branches break into a chuckle, imagine that!

## Secrets Amongst the Spruce

In the woods where squirrels play,
Old pine trees have much to say.
One whispered secrets in my ear,
Like how to dance without a fear.

A raccoon chuckled from a branch,
Said, "Join the trees, it's quite the chance!"
But as I tried to twirl and glide,
I tripped on roots and fell with pride.

The owls hooted in delight,
At my performance on that night.
While critters giggled at my stance,
The forest held its merry dance.

So if you venture in the green,
Beware of dances unseen!
For all the foliage may agree,
You're the star of this comedy.

## Soft Footfalls in the Foliage

With steps that squish like fresh mashed peas,
I tiptoe soft among the trees.
The leaves all rustle, whisper low,
"Hey human, careful, watch your toe!"

A pinecone rolls and takes a leap,
I nearly tripped, it's quite a creep!
The squirrels laugh, they find it grand,
As I perform my clumsy stand.

I laugh along with every thud,
As tree trunks watch me land in mud.
Yet every slip, each joyful tread,
Brings laughter from the woods instead.

So if you walk where shadows loom,
Prepare to face the forest's gloom.
But know with every slip you take,
You share a joke that trees now make.

## Journey through the Needle Carpet

A carpet soft beneath my feet,
Each step a tickle, not a feat.
The needles press like tiny cushions,
Who knew they'd hold such fun-impressions?

I prance through pines, a wobbly thing,
Bouncing like a pogo spring.
The creatures peek from leafy shade,
At my ridiculous parade.

With every twist and silly spin,
The forest whispers with a grin.
The branches sway, they shake with glee,
As I perform my nature spree.

So tread with joy, oh woodland friends,
For laughter here, it never ends.
Just watch your step, and if you fall,
The trees will catch you, after all!

## The Forest's Whispering Veins

In the woods where laughter flows,
The trees engage in friendly prose.
A squirrel shared a fable quick,
Of how I slipped—oh, what a trick!

The roots all chuckled with delight,
While branches waved to greet the night.
Every twig had tales to spin,
Of silly humans tripping in!

I danced among the ferns so green,
With moves that made the pines turn keen.
And as I leapt, a pinecone flew,
Hitting me square—oh, what a view!

So in the forest, take your time,
With giggles from each tree and climb.
For in this grove of jovial shades,
You'll find the joy that nature trades.

## Shadows of the Evergreen

In the forest so wild, a squirrel did dance,
With acorns like marbles, he took a chance.
A pinecone rebellion, the birds flew away,
Laughing at antics of that furry ballet.

Beneath boughs above, the shadows did play,
Whispers of mischief in branches at sway.
A deer with a hat, and a rabbit with shoes,
In the bewildering woods, they can't lose.

## **Trails of Soft Green**

On trails of soft green, the laughter does flow,
Dancing through trees, with a comical show.
A chipmunk in shades, looking sharp as a knife,
Claims he's the king of this woodland life.

Fallen logs become thrones to the wise,
With owls in the crown, they all seem to rise.
But when the wind gusts, the hats start to fly,
Oh, which squeaky critter shall give it a try?

## **Echoes in the Thicket**

In thickets so dense, an echo rings clear,
A raccoon with rhythm, a beat of good cheer.
He fumbles and tumbles, the leaves all around,
As laughter bursts forth from the fairies unbound.

The fox joins the fun, with a wink and a grin,
Declares, "This is how we get dinner in!"
Yet when they all trip on the roots in their tracks,
Together they tumble, all laughter no snacks.

## **Beneath Nature's Embrace**

Beneath nature's embrace, a party unfolds,
With creatures and critters, all daring and bold.
A hedgehog, a turtle, throw a fancy affair,
With disco balls made of the fluff from the air.

The waltz to the bushes, a tango on moss,
The fireflies twinkle, no one feels the loss.
And when night falls softly, they rally around,
To come up with stories, woodland's lost sound.

## Beneath the Conifer's Touch

Under the trees where squirrels play,
I tripped over roots in a silly way.
The pines do giggle, their needles tease,
As I stumble onward, bringing them glee.

Frogs croak a rhythm, so quirky and loud,
While birds chirp gossip, forming a crowd.
A curious raccoon just gave me a wink,
Said he knows more than I in a blink!

There's a trail marked with footprints of glee,
But watch out for puddles, they'll welcome thee.
I slid like a penguin, oh what a sight,
With laughter surrounding, everything's right.

A pinecone rolled over, like a little car,
I raced it for fun, but it traveled far.
The forest is sticky with laughter and game,
With stories that bend, yet always the same.

## Hidden Ways in Nature's Lullaby

In a whispering green, the trees seem to chat,
While I navigate paths, avoiding a cat.
The branches all wave in a breezy delight,
As I dodge a low branch, what a comical sight!

Moss carpets wink, saying 'Come take a seat',
But my behind meets the ground, oh what a feat!
A raccoon nearby just rolls with the laugh,
As I gather my pride, checking my path.

The critters conspire in a woodland ballet,
With owls giving side-eye, 'What's wrong with her sway?'
A pinecone pirouette – oh, what a bold star!
It thuds on my head; I'm just not that far!

Nature rolls chuckles like waves on the shore,
As I step on a twig that decides to encore.
Each trip and each tumble just helps me to see,
That laughter in woods is true company.

## Sylvan Musings

In the shade where the leaves dance, I take a stroll,
But the roots have a plan, to make me lose control.
Beneath the tall pines, I wiggle and sway,
With some very real hopes I won't just decay.

The chipmunks conspire, plotting my fall,
While branches overhead seem to giggle and call.
With acorns like missiles, they drop with a thump,
I leap like a deer; oh, nature loves a jump!

A dandelion sneezed, I'm shocked by the blast,
Who knew fluff could tickle? Who knew it would last?
I tumble and roll, the forest in fits,
As I swat at the pollen, and dodge invisible hits.

The sun peeks through branches, playful and grand,
Encouraging each path, both silly and planned.
With each furry creature to share in my cheer,
The woods are a playground, of laughter sincere!

## Trails of the Tranquil Woods

Strolling down trails, my balance is slick,
I find every branch is a possible trick.
With pine trees applauding and whispers astound,
They chuckle as I leave my dignity on the ground.

A squirrel skitters past, he's stealing my snack,
Daring me onward, while peeking back.
Each splash of the stream sings a comical tone,
As I dance with the frogs, who clearly have grown.

The ground feels like jelly; am I on the moon?
As lays on a log that creaks like a tune.
With laughter from birds who perch on my hat,
I wave with a grin, can't help but chat.

So here in the woods, where goofiness reigns,
Each step is a stumble; each fall breaks the chains.
The laughter is endless, just like the trees,
Wandering here, I find joy, if you please!

## The Tread of Nature's Carpet

Beneath my feet, the forest's sway,
A carpet green where squirrels play.
Each crunch and crack, a joke to share,
As sticks jump out, a prankster's lair.

My shoes now host a pinecone dance,
In every step, I lose my chance.
To walk with grace, it just won't do,
Nature giggles, and I trip too!

So here I am, a bumbling clown,
While trees above wear leafy crowns.
They laugh along with every fall,
As laughter echoes through it all.

In each misstep, a giggle grows,
Along this trail, where whimsy flows.
Nature's jest, I can't outrun,
In this pine paradise, we have fun!

## Through the Thicket's Embrace

The thicket hugs, a leafy mate,
This prickly ball, my shuffling fate.
I swear I saw a rabbit grin,
As branches from the trees begin!

A twist, a turn, I must confess,
This thicket surely stirs distress.
The vines conspire to pull me back,
I laugh aloud, what else to lack?

But nature's arms can hold me tight,
While bushes whisper jokes tonight.
I dance through greens, quite out of breath,
In this embrace of leafy depth.

The way is wild, the laughter's loud,
As critters scurry, oh so proud.
With every snag, a laugh we share,
Through thickets deep, without a care!

## **Sunlight's Flicker on Soft Ground**

Sunlight flickers like a game,
On squishy floor, I lose my name.
Each shadow plays a trick or two,
As whispers dance, and squawks ensue!

The ground below, a sponge of glee,
Where every step begs, "Let's be free!"
I stumble once, and then a twice,
The floor laughs back, oh, isn't it nice?

Mushrooms smile in the golden rays,
As grasshoppers jump in tight ballet plays.
I skip along, my heart so light,
Beneath the sun, the world feels right.

With every laugh, the shadows cheer,
Sunshine giggles, "Come right near!"
So, dance and laugh on this ground so bright,
Where mischief twinkles in soft, warm light!

## The Way of the Winding Trail

The trail winds like a toddler's toy,
With bumps and curves, oh what a joy!
I trip, I tumble, roll on the grass,
The squirrels cheer me as I pass.

Each bend I take feels like a wink,
While pine needles giggle and clink.
"Come join the fun!" they seem to call,
As I leap up, only to fall!

Round and round, there's laughter found,
The trees are clapping all around.
I wave at them, not one to pout,
On this winding route, I dance about!

At every turn, a chuckle waits,
From feathered friends and furry mates.
With every jolt, my grin expands,
On this wild trail, where joy commands!

## The Green Embrace of Stillness

In a forest thick with whispers bright,
I tripped on roots in mid-flight.
The squirrels laughed, oh what a sight,
As I danced away, my pants took flight.

A pine cone fell, a hit so sly,
It bounced and rolled—oh my, oh my!
The trees just shook, no need to cry,
As I laughed, it was worth a try.

Beneath the boughs, I found a seat,
With pine nut pie—a savory treat.
But ants marched in, it was quite a feat,
I shared my slice, though they ate quite neat.

So here I dwell, in this green embrace,
With woodland critters in a funny race.
In the stillness, lots of space,
For a giggle and a snooze, what a perfect place!

## A Dance on Nature's Quilt

In a meadow bright with colors grand,
I tripped and tumbled, fell on the land.
The daisies chuckled, they tried to stand,
As I wobbled up, unplanned and unplanned.

A rooster squawked with a comical flair,
As I attempted a ballerina's air.
The bees joined in, buzzing everywhere,
But I lost my balance, oh how I despair!

With dandelions as my stage so wide,
I pirouetted with arms open wide.
But a passing breeze gave me quite a ride,
And I landed in mud, oh what a slide!

Among the flowers, my dance is done,
The critters are rolling, it's all in fun.
In nature's quilt, we laugh and run,
With every tumble, more joy is spun!

## Ripple of the Silent Woods

In the woods where quiet lingers long,
I spotted a critter, singing a song.
With a leap and a bound, he looked so strong,
But slipped on a pine cone—oh, how wrong!

The moss was thick, a bed so plush,
I thought I'd land with a gentle hush.
But I fell in deep—what a sudden rush!
The chipmunks giggled, my face all flushed.

The shadows danced, the leaves took flight,
As I twirled around, feeling quite right.
Then a twig snapped, oh what a fright,
I vanished in foliage, gone from sight!

But here in this wood, the laughter stays,
With critters around me, we'll play for days.
In the rippling silence, our humor sways,
Nature's charm, in funny ways!

## **Memories in the Pine Dust**

In a clearing filled with needles and shade,
I found a treasure that nature made.
A tangle of twigs, oh! What a trade,
For a game of charades, how I've played!

A breeze arrived with a cheeky grin,
It tossed my hat, and here comes my twin.
The chipmunks giggled, let the fun begin,
As I chased my hat, feeling quite thin.

We built a camp with trunks piled high,
But shadows played tricks; oh, how they lie!
A pine needle pillow made my head sigh,
Yet a prickle of laughter made time fly.

Here nestled deep, in pine dust so fine,
In every tickle, I'm sure I'll shine.
With memories made, I toast with wine,
Nature's funny charm, forever entwined!

## Tapestry of Evergreen Dreams

In the woods, where squirrels play,
I tripped on roots, oh what a day!
The pine cones scattered with a clatter,
As I pondered if my shoes would flatter.

Beneath the boughs, I found my grin,
A bird swooped down, stole my snack, oh sin!
With laughter echoing among the trees,
I ran, arms flailing, in the breeze.

Chasing shadows, I danced a jig,
But stepped on something, felt quite big!
A pile of leaves, or a sneaky toad?
Nature's pranks could fill a road.

Yet each tumble brings a tale to share,
With friends who laugh, all worries bare.
In this tapestry of green delight,
Every wrong step feels just right.

## Wandering through Nature's Melody

Stumbling 'neath the leafy crown,
I swear I saw a squirrel drown!
Not in water, but in surprise,
He nearly leapt; oh, what a rise!

The wind whistled a funny tune,
A raccoon snickering at high noon.
I waved to flowers, said 'good day',
They wilted fast and turned away!

Breezy whispers told me jokes,
The rocks all whispered 'See the folks?'
I couldn't help but join the fun,
And laughed until I saw the sun.

With every step, a giggle shared,
The forest creatures, unprepared.
A symphony of chuckles bright,
In nature's rhythm, pure delight.

## Curves of the Coniferous Trail

Round and round, the timber twists,
I swear I met a tree that wished.
With branches waving, 'Hello!' it cried,
I bowed in honor, took it in stride.

Frogs in the creek were crooning songs,
While bugs joined in and hummed along.
I tried to dance, but slipped and fell,
The laughter echoed, all was well.

A pinecone took a daring leap,
I clapped and cheered, my laughter deep.
It rolled and tumbled 'neath my feet,
Oh, what a day, oh, what a treat!

Despite the stumbles, I pranced with glee,
Among the pines, just nature and me.
Every curve, a twist of fate,
A joke wrapped up by the forest gate.

## The Forest's Gentle Pulse

In the woods, the laughter flows,
Like streams you find where sunshine glows.
I met a leaf that scolded me,
For stepping on its cousin's spree!

The shrubs all giggled as I passed,
'Move along, your shadow's vast!'
With every rustle, a poke, a tease,
Nature's whim was sure to please.

Ants marched like tiny soldiers bold,
With sticks and crumbs, their treasures to hold.
I tried to join, but fell in line,
Right on my face, how divine!

The forest throbbed with happy cheer,
A symphony of joy, Oh dear!
In every step, a dance to prance,
Life's gentle pulse, a funny chance.

## Serenity among the Spruce

Beneath the trees, I found a seat,
With squirrels dancing on my feet.
A chipmunk stole my sandwich, oh,
At least I have my picnic show!

Birds are chirping, a comic line,
They mimic me, it's quite divine!
A gentle breeze, it plays a prank,
And sends my hat down to the bank.

The sun peeks in to smile and tease,
As branches sway with utmost ease.
Nature's laughter fills the air,
While I just sit and have a stare.

Oh what a joy, this silly scene,
With all the greens, it feels like spring!
I laugh at trees with quirky bends,
In the woods, they are my friends!

## A Mosaic of Pine and Light

Sunlight dapples on the ground,
Where tiny creatures dance around.
A spider spins a web with flair,
And traps my toe—oh, what despair!

A pinecone rolls, it starts to race,
And I just chuckle at the pace.
The woodland critters stop and stare,
At my astonished, frozen glare.

With squirrels plotting mischief sly,
They hide my keys as I walk by.
Oh woodland life, so full of cheer,
With leafy laughter all I hear.

The shadows stretch, the sun dips down,
I sport a leaf as my new crown.
Nature's fun is wild and free,
A timeless play, just wait and see!

## Between Silence and Shadows

In quiet woods where critters play,
A raccoon waves as I stray.
He tips his hat, what a surprise,
With twinkling mischief in his eyes!

The owls hoot jokes in muffled tone,
As I trip over my own phone.
"Look at that human!" they all say,
In shadows deep, I laugh away.

The sun dips low, the night creeps near,
And frogs start croaking, loud and clear.
I join their chorus, what a sight!
Merriment dances in the night.

A rustling pine whispers my name,
And in this whisper, there's no shame.
With every step, the laughter grows,
In nature's arms, I strike a pose!

## **Pinecone Dreams on the Earth**

Lying back on a bed of green,
I dream of food—it's quite obscene!
A pinecone plops right on my nose,
And makes me laugh in scruffy clothes.

The ants are busy—oh, what a race!
They've got a banquet, look at their pace!
Each morsel lifted, so carefully,
While I just munch my mystery.

The branches sway, they tease my hair,
And I pretend I do not care.
A shadow moves, it gives me fright,
But it's just a cricket, full of delight.

In this realm of whimsy and cheer,
I find the joy in each strange sphere.
So here I lay, in giggles' throng,
With dreams of pine, where I belong!

## Veins of the Verdant Earth

In shoes too big, I took a stride,
Tripping o'er roots, I barely bide.
The leaves they laughed, a rustling choir,
As I tangled up, my socks caught fire!

A squirrel mockingly stole my hat,
While I danced with a sneaky cat.
Those twigs and brambles play their tricks,
I think this route needs better picks!

My GPS says it's right ahead,
But all I see is a big, old shed.
A forest maze, I'm stuck within,
Is this a hike, or a comedy spin?

With pinecones dropping, I do a jig,
Avoiding ants that seem too big.
Each step a giggle, each turn a gaffe,
Next time I'll bring my better half!

## Through the Whispering Woods

The trees all chuckle, it seems to me,
As branches wave like they're fancy free.
I thought I'd stroll a path so divine,
But found a branch that broke my spine!

A raccoon gave me a judging glance,
As I slipped and started to prance.
Mushrooms looked like they might just say,
Try skipping here, it's a funny play!

The owls hoot jokes in the dead of night,
While I startle, thinking it's a fright.
With twigs as my bandmates, what a sight,
In this whimsy woods, I'm feeling light!

But wait, what's that? A spider parade!
I dance right out; it's not a charade.
Through mirthful whispers, I waddle and trot,
This trip, my dear friends, is quite a plot!

## **Footprints on the Green Canvas**

Step by step, I paint my trail,
With twigs and rocks like a silly tale.
If only my feet would cooperate,
Instead, I bounce like a rubber mate!

Each footfall leaves a mark so bold,
Yet here I find my shoe's been sold.
Now one foot's bare and one's got flair,
A fashion statement, if one would dare!

Ladybugs laugh as I trip and swirl,
While butterflies join in to give a whirl.
Squirrels gather for my grand parade,
But all they want is to watch the charade!

With each pitter-patter on the ground,
A quirky ballet is winding 'round.
My march is silly, my style a tease,
In this green canvas, I'm doing as I please!

## **Cradle of the Pine Essence**

In a cradle made of needles and bark,
I thought I'd nap, but heard a lark.
"Wake up!" it chirps, "Don't be so lazy!
Get on your feet, it's a forest crazy!"

Bouncing from bush to a rock so round,
I'm a circus act on this forest ground.
Pine-scented giggles fill the air,
Even the mushrooms seem to share!

With a bear's grin, I take a dive,
But all I find is a squirrel with a vibe.
He shows me the ropes, a funny little bro,
While I fumble and flail, putting on a show!

As sunset draws, the fireflies gleam,
I trip on roots, and laugh like a dream.
In this charming cradle, all is well,
Just me and laughter, the forest's spell!

## Whispers Beneath the Evergreen

A squirrel with nuts, oh what a sight,
He hears my steps and takes to flight.
Chasing shadows, slipping and tripping,
He laughs at my fall, I'm not quite flipping.

The branches sway, a gentle sway,
As pinecones drop, they steal my play.
I swear I heard a tree bark back,
"Pick up your pace, or face my snack!"

A whisper floats in the scented air,
"Who's that guy with the messy hair?"
I turn around, they snicker loud,
Even the owls this time are proud.

The sun dips low, my legs feel tired,
I'd tell a joke, but I'm so wired.
With whispers soft, the trees all jest,
This nature walk, it's quite the quest!

## Shadows Dancing on Forest Floors

The shadows waltz, a lively bunch,
They do a jig, then take a lunch.
With acorns tossed and laughter loud,
I trip on roots, can't join their crowd.

A rabbit hops in a spiffy suit,
"Join my dance!" he shouts, oh what a hoot!
With every twist and every turn,
My footing fades, oh how I yearn!

The owls join in with a wise old grin,
As squirrels cheer with a nutty spin.
But I just stumble, laugh and fall,
Oh, lend me grace, just once, not all!

The night wraps round, a sparkling cloak,
A chorus of giggles, oh what a poke!
The forest sways, and I'm all in,
With shadows dancing, I can't help but grin.

## Journey Among the Tall Pines

With tall pines looming, I start my quest,
"Look out for bears!" they jest, I guess.
But all I see are trees and glee,
No grizzly bears, just pine-scented spree.

There's a chipmunk who thinks he's the king,
With tiny paws, he's ready to fling.
"Come dance!" he squeaks as he makes a dash,
I'd rather munch on my snack stash!

The breeze is playful, it tugs my hat,
Away it goes – now how about that?
I chase it down, I stumble and slide,
As laughter rings, can't fight the tide.

But with each step, I'm having a ball,
Nature's a stage and I'm on call.
So here I go, through branches wide,
Among the tall pines, I'll take a ride!

## **Trails of Fragrant Green**

Through trails so green, I skip and hop,
The scent of pine makes my heart plop.
As birds above sing their silly tune,
I join in loud, like a cartoon!

The squirrels chime in with a nutty cheer,
"Who needs a map? Just follow the deer!"
Yet every detour stirs in my laugh,
A game of chase through nature's path.

A twig snaps loud, I freeze in place,
A deer pops out with a curious face.
"Is this a party? I've come to play!"
I nod my head, let's dance away!

With every turn, a new surprise,
The laughter echoes to the skies.
In fragrant greens, my heart takes flight,
This silly journey feels just right!

# The Allure of the Hidden Glade

Under the trees, we scamper about,
While squirrels judge our clumsy route.
A slip here, a fall there, what a delight,
We laugh till we cry, what a silly sight!

Mushrooms wink from their leafy beds,
Whispering secrets to our heads.
We dance with shadows, so carefree,
A waltz with the wind, oh so wild and free!

Who knew ferns could be such good friends?
They poke and prod as the laughter blends.
In this glade full of laughter and cheer,
We lose our worries, and all else disappears!

So let's embrace this wooded shenanigan,
With every misstep, we're having a blast again.
For nature's secret, fun-filled scene,
Is where we'll frolic, oh so serene!

## Lost in the Needle Embrace

Tripping on pine cones, oh what a joke,
I swear this root just tried to provoke!
Branches scratch and giggle with glee,
As we tumble down like a family tree!

Underfoot, carpeted miracles grow,
While bees buzz by, putting on a show.
"Is that a flower or just a disguise?"
Nature's prankster, it's no surprise!

We crawl through the fuzz and make new friends,
Acorns and twigs, oh how the fun extends!
Frogs croak behind bushes, keeping score,
Ribbiting loudly, "What's in store?"

In this needle embrace, we're forever lost,
Laughing and slipping, oh, what a cost!
With laughter as fuel, we twirl and we spin,
This joyful madness, our adventure begins!

## The Heartbeat of the Forest Floor

Hear that thump? It's our shoe on a stone,
Echoing laughter, not quite alone.
With every leap, our soles get quite sore,
While giggles rise up from the cozy floor!

Each step we take, little creatures scatter,
With buggy little eyes staring in chatter.
"Are they friends or foes?"—what a funny scheme,
We'll take our chances, let's chase and scream!

Crickets serenade as we dance in delight,
To the rhythm of branches creaking at night.
Watch out, old tree! You're not down for the count,
As we climb, slip, and find our own amount.

In this secret place, the heart truly sings,
With giggles and chatter echoing things.
So here's to the woodland, our whimsical shore,
Shuffling through laughter on the forest floor!

## Echoing Traces in the Green

With every step, a crunching sound,
Echoes of laughter bounce all around.
Is that you or a squirrel on the run?
Nature's a comedy—we're here just for fun!

Under the branches, the mischief brews,
With slippery moss and adventurous views.
As we jump and yell, "Look at me now!"
The forest responds with a soft, "Oh wow!"

Twigs underfoot create a symphony,
Playing our tune, a wild cacophony.
Our antics leave marks, like joyous graffiti,
In echoing traces, we're totally witty!

So here in the green, let's frolic and play,
With giggles and grins, we'll twist the day.
With every misstep, we cherish our spree,
In echoes of laughter, we dance with glee!

## The Dance of Shadows and Light

Beneath the trees, shadows play,
Dancing limbs in a bright ballet.
Squirrels groove to a raucous beat,
While chipmunks boogie on tiny feet.

A sunbeam dips, a tree trunk spies,
As owls hoot loud with wide, wise eyes.
Critters chuckle in leafy lanes,
Echoing laughter of joyful refrains.

Trees sway side to side, what a show,
With forest folks putting on a glow.
The wind joins in with a gentle whoosh,
While bugs buzz around in a silly swoosh.

Oh look, the mushrooms tap their toes,
In a fanciful dance that nobody knows.
Nature's party never seems to stop,
As shadows jiggle and sunlight hops!

## An Invitation to the Forest's Quiet

Hear that whisper in the air?
A tree just told me there's a bear!
But wait, it's just a twig that cracked,
As all the forest critters relaxed.

Squirrels argue over the best acorn,
While frogs claim the leaf that they adorn.
The silence hums with a subtle thrill,
Nature's humor is a quiet skill.

Mice hold court with their tiny squeaks,
While undercover lizards play hide-and-seek.
And if you listen with careful glee,
You might hear the trees whisper a punny decree!

An invitation to find some glee,
In a world where chaos just flees.
Come join the fun, but don't be late,
Or miss the laughter of nature's fate!

## Whispers Beneath the Canopy

Under leaves, secrets softly blend,
With giggles shared by each furry friend.
A fox tells tales with a teasing wink,
While hedgehogs sip on a fruity drink.

Pine trees gossip, their needles swish,
As rabbits hop in a playful dish.
Even the mushrooms lift a cap,
Chiming in for a woodland clap.

Beetles roll leaves as if they're gold,
While butterflies boast of adventures bold.
The forest floor's a stage of wit,
Where every critter's a perfect fit.

Whispers echo tales of the absurd,
As laughter dances with every word.
In this shady realm, there's much to cheer,
Join the laughter, for fun is here!

## Secrets of the Forest Floor

Down below, where roots intertwine,
A party erupts, and it's simply divine.
Ants march out in a parade so neat,
To celebrate in a furry retreat.

Raccoons in masks act so mysterious,
While worms plot schemes that sound quite delirious.
Toadstools gossip and giggles erupt,
As the underbrush welcomes, 'Hey, come on up!'

Lizards play chess—oh, such a sight!
As bees buzz by with pure delight.
The forest floor, such a vibrant scene,
Teaches us all to laugh in between.

Secrets keep blooming, oh what a floor!
Where laughter bounces and spirits soar.
Nature's joke book is always a score,
In this silly haven, we can't ask for more!

## Songs of the Suburban Sylvan

In the woods where squirrels dance,
They argue over crumbs of chance.
With acorns flying through the air,
The chase turns into a woodland fair.

A raccoon steals a garden hose,
While bunnies wear the latest clothes.
They prance about in dapper suits,
While foxes plot their veggie hoots.

From trees that sway with a sigh,
The cedar whispers a cheeky lie.
"Don't mind the wind," it seems to say,
"Life's better when you play all day!"

In this green realm where laughs abound,
You'll trip on roots, then be spellbound.
With every stumble, giggles rise,
In suburban woods, there's no disguise.

## The Arboreal Embrace of Solitude

Under branches, quiet waits,
While chipmunks argue silly fates.
One claims he saw a UFO,
The other just wants popcorn, though!

Amidst the trunks, a lone owl spies,
A slip of socks – what a surprise!
With each soft hoot, it shakes its head,
"Oh humans, why can't you be fed?"

In solitude, the big pine grins,
While beetles hold their dance-off wins.
They shimmy underneath the bark,
In a contest that's quite the lark!

The breeze confides in quirky tones,
As laughter mingles with the stones.
In nature's silence, jokes abound,
A punchline lives in every sound.

## **Secrets in the Sunlight's Flicker**

The sun peeks through, a winking light,
As shadows dance in playful flight.
A moth complains of burdens big,
While ants march on, oh so sprig!

A lizard sunbathes, striking poses,
While a wise old toad does his dozes.
"Hurry not, keep drama at bay,"
Sings a cricket, "Join my cabaret!"

With secrets held beneath the leaves,
The bushes chuckle as one deceives.
"Did you hear about the gossip vine?
It's blanketed under a pine!"

The forest hums with tales untold,
Of wildwood shenanigans so bold.
In sunlight's flicker, laughter thrives,
As nature spins its tales of lives.

## In the Arms of the Evergreen

Beneath the arms of a tree so stout,
The saplings chatter, filled with doubt.
"Are we plants, or just tree wishes?
I hear those foxes make great dishes!"

With needles dropping like confetti,
Two pinecones argue who's the petty.
"Just drop it now, all's well in jest,
At least we're not a gourmet pest!"

In evergreen arms, they plot and scheme,
While birds above begin to dream.
"What if we take that squirrel's hat?
Can we? Shall we? Oh, imagine that!"

Giggling softly in the shade,
Each creature crafting a parade.
In nature's arms, their spirits sing,
Creating laughter, their favorite thing.

## Soundtrack of the Subtle Breeze

Whispers of wind play their sweet tune,
As squirrels dance madly under the moon.
Pinecones drop like confetti rain,
Each thud brings laughter, not a hint of pain.

The rustle of needles, a giggling sound,
Nature's humor, all around.
Birds chirp jokes in a feathery choir,
As I trip on a root, my mood climbs higher.

**In the Lull of the Evergreens**

Tall tales of trees in a woodland hush,
With friendly shadows in a gentle rush.
The branches wave as if to say,
"Join the fun, don't just pass by today!"

Each step feels fluffy, a tickling spree,
Like walking on clouds, so carefree.
The pines chuckle softly, I hear their plea,
"Don't mind the squirrels, they're just like thee!"

## Journeying to the Unknown Clearing

Where do these footsteps hope to go?
Through tangled brush where the wild things grow.
Every twist and turn, an unsure fate,
Who knew a stroll could be this great?

The sun seems to wink, a mischievous friend,
Leading me on, but I can't pretend.
I trip on a twig, oh what a sight!
Gravity giggles, my balance takes flight!

## Softness Beneath Each Step

A carpet of needles, soft and round,
Invites my feet to dance on the ground.
With each little shuffle, there's laughter and glee,
As a chorus of critters join in with me.

The pine trees sway in a gentle embrace,
Their limbs seem to laugh, oh, what a place!
Beneath every branch, a chuckle awaits,
In this jolly realm, it's pure, silly fate.

## Lingering in the Wooded Dream

Underneath the lush green veil,
Squirrels plot their nutty trail.
Branches creak with all their might,
While birds debate who sings just right.

Mushrooms flaunt their colorful hats,
As rabbits gossip with the spats.
If trees could laugh, oh what a scene,
The woods would dance, so fresh, so keen!

Fog rolls in just for fun,
Transforming trails from one to none.
The sun peeks, then ducks away,
Playing hide and seek all day!

In here, where magic likes to bloom,
Nature's jesters frolic in the gloom.
Every corner hides a cheer,
In this dreamy, wooded sphere.

## Ribbons of the Resilient Pines

Pine trees don their green capes,
Swishing like they're in escape.
They sway and giggle in the breeze,
Whispering secrets with such ease.

A pinecone rolls, it makes a dash,
While bunnies hop with boisterous crash.
The needles carpet all around,
A prickly quilt on soft ground.

Tall trunks make silly faces too,
Waving branches, 'Hey! How do you do?'
If you stumble, they just grin,
'Take a seat, let's laugh again!'

In this forest, where antics reign,
Even shadows shout, 'Let's entertain!'
Nature's circus, oh such glee,
With piney friends, we're wild and free!

## Pines and the Poetry of Soil

Beneath the pines, the stories grow,
Worms and beetles dip and flow.
A silly dance, they twirl and spin,
While mushrooms chuckle, 'Let's begin!'

The soil hums a cozy tune,
As ants march out beneath the moon.
They carry crumbs like tiny ships,
With lavish feasts on tiny lips.

Pine needles fall in soft ballet,
Softly saying, 'Come to play!'
Critters gather, all in line,
Ready for the lunch divine!

Each step is filled with giggles bright,
In this soft and funny light.
The forest floor has tales to share,
With every twist, you'd have to stare!

## A Glimpse into the Verdant Mysteries

In the thicket, laughter rings,
As chipmunks play on tiny springs.
Pine trees stand, tall and wise,
Keeping watch with sparkling eyes.

Frogs croak jokes in leaps and bounds,
While owls spin tall stories round.
Underneath their leafy shrouds,
Nature's punchlines form great crowds.

Sunbeams tickle the forest floor,
Where shadows dance, and spirits soar.
Every corner hides a giggle,
In playful leaves, the breezes wiggle.

As dusk descends, the fun won't wane,
Crickets join with a rhythmic gain.
In the woodlands, joy's the key,
Unlocking laughter, wild and free!

## The Quiet Symphony of Pines

In the woods where silence plays,
The trees gossip in funny ways,
A squirrel drops a nut with flair,
And lands it right on my wild hair.

The breeze hums tunes of joy and jest,
While branches wiggle in a dance fest,
A hidden bird takes a cheeky shot,
And plops on my head, it's like a hot pot!

A rabbit hops with a silly grin,
Challenging me to join his spin,
In a mossy patch, we both feel free,
A woodland party, just him and me.

As I step over twigs and leaves,
A chipmunk mocks, oh how he weaves,
With laughter ricocheting through the pines,
In nature's jokes, the humor shines.

## Songs of the Woodland Floor

The ground around is a canvas bright,
Each leaf a note in nature's light,
A plump toad croaks a tune so bold,
While mushrooms dance like stories told.

With each crunch underfoot, my shoes balk,
A chipmunk scolds me, 'You can't just walk!'
A red ant gives me a pointed stare,
Saying, 'Watch it, buddy! You're in my lair!'

The flowers giggle, the brook sings clear,
While beetles roll snacks like a sheer sphere,
I joined their fun, I can't deny,
Waltzing with weeds as the sun says hi.

When the evening falls with a cheeky grin,
The wind plays notes, let the frolics begin,
A concert in the woods, lively and bright,
With laughter echoing 'til the last light.

# Under the Veil of Spruce

Beneath the spruce with a poky crown,
I found a tow-headed acorn clown,
He told me jokes about winter fluff,
'Why wear pants? Just wear enough!'

Twigs dance about, declaring a ballet,
'Join us, come on!' they seem to say,
I trip and tumble, what a proud face,
Finding my rhythm in this green space.

Mice hold auditions for a furry play,
While ants form lines for a cabaret,
In this sprightly glen beneath leafy skies,
The only rule is, giggles defies!

When shadows stretch and the stars peak out,
The woods keep laughing without a doubt,
For here under spruce, fun's our decree,
In a woodland symphony wild and free.

## Glimmers in the Underbrush

In the underbrush where mischief creeps,
Glimmers dance where the sunlight peeks,
A snail in a tux, polished and grand,
Invites me to join his slow-motion band.

Small critters plan a wild parade,
With twigs for drums and leaves they've laid,
A caterpillar plays the kazoo,
And I can't help but tap my shoe!

The brambles chuckle, the flowers sway,
As butterflies flutter in a bright ballet,
In this raucous corner, life plays its part,
With giggles and grins, it warms my heart.

The evening glimmers, laughter stirs,
Even a hedgehog joins with purrs,
In the undergrowth where humor's lush,
Nature's fun fest, in vibrant hush.

## **Gentle Rustle of Forgotten Trails**

In the woods where squirrels dance,
And mushrooms take a daring chance,
I tripped over roots, oh what a sight,
The trees chuckled, 'You don't stand right!'

A raccoon peered with eyes so wide,
Was he judging how I tried to glide?
As I stumbled through a prickly clump,
He snickered, 'Nature's not for the clump.'

Elusive paths with secrets abound,
Where every twist leaves laughter unbound,
I followed ferns that waved hello,
But now I'm lost, oh where did I go?

With every step, I juggle delight,
The sun's peeking through, what a sight,
Though I may trip and take a fall,
The trees just giggle, 'You'll learn it all!'

## A Whisper in the Pine Boughs

Among the pines, a secret's told,
In trails that twist and turn so bold,
A chipmunk grinned as I held tight,
To a branch that wasn't quite right!

Each bough above gently swayed,
As I dodged a sap that waylaid,
'Careful there!' the pinecone said,
'You've got a friendly bump on your head!'

The whispers seemed to tease and cheer,
As I danced along, fueled by fear,
Mischief beckoned, laughter rang,
In this forest, wild joy sang!

Yet as I stumbled, what a ruckus!
Leaves laughed loudly, oh, how they fuss,
With each misstep, I found my groove,
In the pines, I can't help but move!

## Woods of Infinite Journeys

Where paths meander with no end,
And trees around seem quite the friend,
Naughty roots trip my happy feet,
But oh how life's little bumps feel sweet!

With every step, a funny twist,
A fern waved 'hi' and I quite missed,
A squirrel whispered, 'Name your prize!'
I held my snack—what a big surprise!

A sunbeam tickled my curious head,
While beetles held a parade instead,
Their tiny drums beat loud in glee,
Concerts here are always free!

So I'll laugh and dance in this embrace,
Where every stumble finds its place,
In these woods, full of jesting runs,
Nature's laughter is number one!

## The Soft Cradle of Earth

A cozy patch where laughter grows,
Beneath the pines where the wild wind blows,
I tripped on moss, it was a blast,
I'm sure the trees saw me and laughed!

The ground beneath is soft like cake,
But oh, beware the sneaky snake,
It winked at me while I sprawled wide,
'You've got the grace of a walrus slide!'

Sunlight dappled, a whimsical sight,
Each step a giggle, pure delight,
With shouts of joy, the woods respond,
To every tumble, a route to bond!

So I'll tiptoe through this earthly dome,
With pine trees singing, 'Come on home!'
In the cradle of nature, fun's the norm,
In this silly forest, all hearts stay warm!

## Enchanted Greenways

The squirrels play cards, what a sight,
They giggle and chatter, full of delight.
Acorns roll past, a grand parade,
While birds offer snacks, homemade lemonade!

A rabbit wears shades, struts with some flair,
He hops to the beat, with wind in his hair.
The fox joins the dance, tail flowing like silk,
In the forest's own disco, all groove and no milk!

Chipmunks in bow ties, bopping along,
While tree trunks are conduits for their song.
The moss on the ground invites all to sit,
You can't help but laugh at their natural wit!

Between ferns and flowers, it's all quite silly,
With every odd creature, the trail feels so frilly.
A party awaits in the shade of the trees,
Where whimsy's abundant and laughter's a breeze!

## Nature's Woven Pathways

A caterpillar's wearing a tiny top hat,
While bees drive around in a leaf-covered brat.
They honk and they buzz, creating a scene,
In this leafy amusement park, nothing's routine.

Mice gather for tea, sipping dew from the grass,
They toast to the day, raising glasses en masse.
The crickets provide quite the lively tune,
Encouraging all to dance under the moon.

The ants play charades over crumbs on the floor,
And the hedgehogs compete in a squirrel's next door.
Nature's a circus, full of giggles and glee,
Only laughter surrounds, in this vast jubilee!

As fireflies twinkle, it flickers and fades,
But no one seems worried; they're all happy brades.
They skip down the lane, in a feathery race,
As laughter erupts in this wild, leafy place!

## The Sigh of the Old Pines

Old pines stretch and creak, share secrets so wise,
While owls roll their eyes and wear humorous ties.
A family of raccoons throw a wild bash,
They tumble and fumble, all making a splash!

The trees exchange stories, trunk to trunk,
About all their guests, both weird and funk.
The wind whispers jokes to the leaves overhead,
While beetles in bowler hats nod their wise heads.

Woodpeckers tapping like a drumline parade,
While shadows of pinecones hold court in the glade.
The laughter of critters cascades from each branch,
Creating sweet harmony, a whimsical chant.

And so the old pines shake off the dew,
As squirrels scurry by, with much ado.
Each sighing embrace in the sunbeams' soft glow,
Unraveling the giggles that underneath flow!

## Rustic Trails of the Mind

In the woods, I wander, where thoughts prance around,
A rabbit debates with a tree on the ground.
The winds carry whispers, both jolly and cheeky,
While shadows do flips that seem rather freaky.

Mushrooms hold meetings, talk fungi with glee,
While hedgehogs recite poems, sipping on tea.
The brook sings a tune that makes all creatures sway,
As chipmunks crack jokes—you could laugh all day!

Each stump is a seat and the moss is a couch,
To listen to crickets debate with a louch.
In this rustic retreat, nothing's too dire,
When laughter echoes like the crackling fire.

Oh, the magic of nature with friends big and small,
In this zany wild, I feel free for it all.
With thoughts that run wild, and humor so spry,
Who needs paved highways? Just breathe and comply.

www.ingramcontent.com/pod-product-compliance
Lightning Source LLC
Chambersburg PA
CBHW071850160426
43209CB00003B/486